Dedicated to Ina

Thanks for the adventure

Welcome to the Falkland Islands

The Falkland Islands is situated in the South Atlantic and is classed as a British overseas territory.

The islands are home to fantastic wildlife including penguins, sealions and birds. The breath-taking views of nature as well as the small capital Stanley attract thousands of tourists from cruise ships every year.

I hope you enjoy this colouring book I have made using some photos I took whilst living in Stanley from 2019 to 2020. It was an adventure and a great privilege to be part of island life.

WELCOME TO
THE FALKLAND ISLANDS

The cathedral sits near the waterfront with amazing stained glass windows and a beautiful garden to enjoy the sunshine in. the garden is home to the iconic Whalebone Arch that is made from the jawbones of blue whales.

The cathedral also houses some flags, banners and artefacts that tell stories of island life.

CHRIST CHURCH CATHEDRAL

The museum is full of amazing artefacts and experiences from the history of the Falkland's (over 5,000 of them!)

Follow the history of the Falkland Islands from when it first settled in the 1760's ,to the war in 1982, to present day with examples of life in the Falkland Islands for those in camp and those in town.

The gift shop is great for souvenirs and if you feel peckish the teaberry café is perfect for small cakes or a coffee. I recommend the Banoffee Pie but bananas are not available all year round as they are shipped in once a month!

The home of the governor for the Falkland Islands: His Excellency Nigel Phillips CBE.

First built in 1845, it has been the official residence of the governor of the Falklands since the mid 19th century and Sir Ernest Shackleton even stayed here during his famous expedition.

If you are lucky enough to be invited for dinner, lunch or any event here then congratulations. The sausage rolls and canapés are amazing and the gardens are spectacular!

Battle Memorial & Solar System Sculpture Walk

Situated just behind the battle memorial featured right is a sculpture of the sun and the start of the solar system walk around the waters of Stanley harbour and Moody Brook. Follow along the waters edge to find all the sculptures, one for ever planet.

Tips from the walking guide include:

The outer planet models are situated in rocky outcrops at the top of their respective ridge, the exception is Jupiter located on the coast.

Look at the inner planets by the Battle Memorial before setting out to get an idea of what to look for in the hills.

It's a great afternoon's adventure across Stanley.

The waterfront hotel & cafe

The waterfront hotel - beautiful cakes and a great spot for lunch overlooking the water.

The waterfront is situated just near the tourist jetty. You can sit in the front overlooking the water and sample a great meal or just one of their many desserts - I love the banoffee pie but also lookout for local delicacies including teaberry cheesecake!

The restaurant is open for lunch and dinner and the hotel operates all year round with cosy rooms.

Many boats dock along the Stanley waterfront. The Pelagic Australis is currently docked on the tourist jetty as I write this and seals can often be found asleep next to it. Another of our favourite boats to see outside our windows is the Pharos (above in red) which patrols the waters around the Falklands and South Georgia.

BOAT

FALKLAND CONSERVATION

Falkland Conservation is central to sustaining the fantastic nature and wildlife of the Falkland Islands.

You will find their offices right on the waterfront close to the public jetty. They also have a beautiful garden open to the public.

If you are staying a while in the islands then the FIELD GUIDE TO THE PLANTS OF THE FALKLAND ISLANDS is not only a beautiful book but also a great guide to the many plants you will find around the island. The conservation team work within the community with many school visits, public talks and publications. The islands are home to the world's largest breeding populations of Black-browed Albatross and Southern Giant Petrel.

Penguins at cape dolphin

Cape Dolphin - a two hour drive from Stanley, this is one of my favourite places to visit.

It's the most northernly point on the East Island. Penguins are dotted about the large open landscape that you can navigate via a 4x4. There's often a large colony of sealions to look at and the occasional dolphin on the water. The blowhole is a particularly beautiful spot to stop and look out on the ocean with penguins nearby.

Mounted in the middle of Victory Green. The mast is from the first of its kind, a steam ship constructed from iron and screw propelled. It was built in 1843 by Isambard Kingdom Brunel.

She was badly damaged in the Cape Horn gale in 1886 and lay for a long time at Sparrow Cove outside of Stanley before being towed back to Bristol and restored in 1970.

First unveiled on Thatcher Day in 2015, this bust commemorates the life of the UK Prime Minister who had a major role in the Falklands War.

The bust is located next to the war memorial in Stanley on Thatcher Drive. The plaque underneath states words spoken by Margaret Thatcher as Prime Minister on 3rd April 1982.

"They are few in number, but they have the right to live in peace, to choose their own way of life and allegiance.

The statue was made by local sculptor and taxidermist Steve Massam. You can follow him on Instagram where he has lots of other creative projects focused around the wildlife of the Falklands.

Instagram @Steve.massam

MARGARET THATCHER BUST

Stanley is beautiful from the water.

Throughout the year seals, birds and even the occasional dolphin are known to swim past. Take a stroll along the path that runs the entire length or if you can brave the freezing cold take a ride in a kayak.

If you are lucky enough to visit on the 1st January then lookout for the handmade vessels that take part in the annual boat race along the water towards the Narrows Bar. Entertaining fun that the whole town gathers for.

THE WATERFRONT VIEW OF STANLEY

Our magnificent raft named Alexi II, that earned us last place in the raft race 2020 and a wooden spoon as a prize!

An iconic symbol of the Falkland Islands.

Lots of people make the Falkland Islands their home from all around the world. Contractors come to the islands to help in all areas of industry, government including the hospital and education system on the islands.

To link Stanley where most live, people place a small sign (often handmade) to show just how far they are from home.

If you are lucky enough to get to come to the Falklands make sure you place a sign before you leave. Even better if you can get it near to the top!

There are hundreds of signs already in almost every colour from all over the world - how many have you visited?

THE TOTEM POLE

A traditional London route master bus sits by the pier to welcome tourists as they disembark from their cruise ships throughout the summer months.

Its in here that tourists can book trips out to see the brilliant places across the islands such as volunteer point, gypsy cove and other sites populated with penguins.

There are five different types of penguin that make the Falkland Islands their home. They are immortalised on special 50p coins - see if you can collect them all!

CAPE PEMBROKE LIGHTHOUSE

Cape Pembroke lighthouse is a stunning view surrounded by waves and wildlife.

You can get the key from the museum and take a trip up the stairs and ladders to the top on a good day and see far out across all of the waves. The lighthouse no longer operates but is a iconic location for the Falkland's with many events held here including the most southernly park run in the world each weekend.

BOAT

Printed in Great Britain
by Amazon

10386884R00020